Life Happened,

Now What?

By Shalithya Stewart

Dedication

This book is dedicated to every one of you

The seekers…

The inquirers…

The lost…

The found…

The imperfect…

The confused…

The inspired…

The happy…

The sad…

This book is for all because God is so multi-faceted that he can give every one of us the things we need and I believe this book is a token of wisdom that can help, guide, transform, and inspire.

~~ SS ~~

Table of Contents

Life happens to the best of us, regardless of our religious background. Just look around, problems seem to plague us all: fear, doubt, death, sickness, and disease. However, we do not have to accept those things as they happen to us. If you are a believer, there are covenant promises to which we are entitled, but we have to understand what they are and how to access them.

Many of you may be thinking, I attend church and Bible study regularly, why is this happening? If we are going to be victorious over the trials that come, attending church and Bible study is not going to be enough. We are going to have to step it up a notch, a few notches. Some of you may be wondering, "How do I actually accomplish that?" I'm glad you asked. If life has happened and you are asking, "Now what?" Continue to read as I unfold the steps needed for navigating the trials of life and giving you victory.

Step One:
Repent, Start With a Clean Slate

"Repent, then, and turn to God, so that your sins may be wiped out, that times of refreshing may come from the Lord" (Acts 3:19).

You may be thinking, "I have not done anything wrong. Why should I repent?" If we can be honest, we are not perfect, and we all make mistakes daily, whether knowingly or unknowingly.

Context: We have to make sure, as we go before God, that we are blameless, especially when we engage in a spiritual battle. Basically, we want to ensure the enemy has no spiritual legal basis for overtaking us. We need to ask for forgiveness because we sin and fall short of His glory on a daily basis. The following prayer is one example you can use to start with a clean slate.

Prayer: Father God, I come with a repenting heart asking for forgiveness for all sins known and unknown so that my sins may be wiped out and times of refreshing may come. Amen.

Step Two:
Evaluate Your Situation: Count Up the Cost

"Or what king would go to war against another king without first sitting down with his counselors to discuss whether his army of 10,000 could defeat the 20,000 soldiers marching against him?" (Luke 14:31 NLT).

When something major occurs within our lives, instead of allowing our emotions to overwhelm us, take a moment to relax, gather your thoughts, and allow the Holy Spirit to arise. It is only at this point that you will start to gain some form of insight into the matter before you. Once you have calmed yourself, then begin evaluating the situation.

Context: Identify the Who, the What, and the Where:

The Who: Does this issue directly impact you personally, or is it someone close to you, whether it be a spouse, children, or family?

The What: It is difficult to devise a plan to overcome struggles without pinpointing the issue at hand. It may be death, loss, sickness, grief, rebellion, worry, witchcraft, etc.

The Where: At this point, you have established or pinpointed the issue before you. Now, ask God to reveal where this problem or attack originated. Where did this come from? Or what action/behavior or inaction/lack of behavior could have opened the door for this situation to arise?

Now that you have assessed the situation and have identified the Who, What, and Where and repented, you must get understanding, which is the next step in overcoming the situations life may throw your way.

Step 3: Get Understanding

"Wisdom is the principle thing, therefore, get wisdom and in all thy getting, get understanding" (Proverbs 4:7 KJV).

Context: Wisdom is having enlightenment, insight, or possessing a wise outlook on a situation, which will lead to understanding. Once you gain an understanding of a thing or situation, it often brings about peace. Not only is it important to gain a general understanding of the issue you're facing, but it is also vital to understand who you are spiritually and who you belong to.

Understanding Who You Are and Whose You Are

"But you are a chosen people, a royal priesthood, a holy nation, God's special possession, that you may declare the praises of him who called you out of darkness into his wonderful light" (1 Peter 2:9).

Context: Having a solid understanding not only of who you are in God but who you belong to helps set the tone for how you respond to challenges as they come about throughout life. According to the scripture, we are the chosen people of God. It is something to be chosen, picked out, or selected as being the best or most appropriate of elected people. When you are chosen, you have to understand that you are very special to God. He has set you apart specifically for Himself, and there is nothing He will not do for you, including giving you access to His power.

You must also understand that when you are chosen by God, spiritual attacks are inevitable because you possess something that can destroy your enemies, and they are threatened by who you are now as well as who you will become. Attacks become more frequent or evident when:

- Growing in the knowledge of God
- A prophetic word is given
- Starting something new
- Elevating to a new level in God

These are just a few examples of when the enemy will try and set you back. However, as you gain clarity of who God says you are, you will begin to walk in His power, which is the anointing.

Understanding Your Access

"I have given you authority to trample on snake and scorpions and to overcome all the power of the enemy, nothing will harm you" (Luke 10:19 NIV).

Context: When problems arise, most people become concerned, nervous, or have no insight on how to respond. Once you truly understand the level of power you have access to, doubt, fear, and uncertainty will take a backseat. You have access to the greatest source of power, which is the word of God. As the scripture states, you have authority, which means permission and the ability to walk over (dominate) snakes and scorpions, as well as defeat every power of the enemy, and no harm shall touch you in the process. God has set you up to win and to have a sure victory over every attack that comes upon your life. You must believe and have faith in the words God has spoken, as well as have faith that you can carry out these things with God leading the way.

Key Note

"When you are going through something, whether it be loss, hurt, lack, etc., you will experience VARIOUS emotions, but what must remain CONSTANT is the word of God over the situation."

Step Four: Have Unshakable Faith

"Now faith is the substance of things hoped for, the evidence of things not yet seen" (Hebrews 11:1 KJV).

Context: Faith is having complete trust and confidence in God. You have to believe that whatever situation or problem you may be facing will change because you believe in God and His word. When circumstances come, you must know that as you submit the situation to God through strategic prayer, He will answer. You must believe in the ability and power God has provided.

"For as the body without the spirit is dead, so faith without works is dead also" (James 2:26 KJV).

Context: Just having faith alone will not produce the results you desire. Sometimes, faith requires movement. You have to be active in your faith by stepping out into the unknown at times without having all the answers. As you move forward and grow in faith, you should aspire to have unshakable faith.

"³And when the centurion heard of Jesus, he sent some Jewish elders to him, requesting him to come and make his bond servant well.⁶ And Jesus went with them. But when he was not far from the house, the centurion sent [some] friends to Him saying Lord, do not trouble [Yourself], for I am not sufficiently worthy to have You come under my roof;⁷ Neither did I consider myself worthy to come to You. But [just] speak a word, and my servant boy will be healed ⁹ Now when Jesus heard this, He marveled at him, and He turned and said to the crowd that followed Him, I tell you, not even in [all] Israel have I found such great faith [as this]. ¹⁰ And when the messengers who had been sent returned to the house, they found the bond servant who had been ill quite well again" (Luke 7: 3, 6-7, 9-10 AMP).

Context: This is an excellent example of unshakable faith. The centurion understood the level of authority that Jesus carried, and he believed. You, too, must take God at His word. When it feels like you are pressed on all sides, meaning even if it seems there is chaos at home, church, or work, and everything seems to be falling apart, and everyone is acting up, let your faith arise. As we step out, God honors the movement and will give insight on the way. So, seek the divine authority of the Lord that is found in God's word. Since the word of God has great authority, you must also speak His word over your situation and watch things shift in your favor.

Step Five: Weaponize Your Mouth

"Death and life are in the power of the tongue, and those who love it and indulge it will eat its fruit and bear the consequences of their words" (Proverbs 18:21 AMP).

Context: One of the most vital lessons you can learn is that your mouth is a powerful weapon. We have the authority to speak life into a situation, but we also have the power to speak death. You have to be careful of the words you speak, especially when you are going through tough, uncertain times. The outcome and severity of circumstances can be determined by the words you speak. Begin to change how you talk! When you speak or pray the word of God over situations, the very foundations of the world shake.

"And at midnight Paul and Silas sang praises unto God: and the prisoners heard them. And suddenly there was a great earthquake, so that, the foundations of the prison were shaken and immediately all the doors were opened and everyone's bands were loosed" (Acts 16:25-26 KJV).

Context: Just as Paul and Silas used their mouths to speak in a mighty way through prayer over their experience, you must do the same. Your mouth is like a portal through which God's power flows. Now that you understand how powerful the words that come out of your mouth are, you must begin to speak to the mountain in your life.

Step 6: Speak to Your Mountain

"I assure you and most solemnly say to you, whoever says to the mountain, be lifted up and thrown into the sea! And does not doubt in his heart [God's unlimited power], but believes that what he says is going to take place, it will be done for him [in accordance with God's will]" (Mark 11:23 AMP).

Context: What are you declaring over your life and situation? When things, people, or circumstances stand against you, you should speak to that particular issue, as stated in the above scripture. If you are wondering how, it is very simple. Take the current situation and find scriptures related to the issue you are facing. Don't worry; you can do this even if you are not a Bible scholar. The following are a couple of ways you can find those scriptures:

- Look in the back of your Bible. There is usually a list of scriptures separated into categories, such as wisdom, grief, worry, anger, etc. Find the category that applies.

- Search with Google or any search engine browser for scriptures related to the situation, e.g., forgiveness. Search: Scriptures on forgiveness.

Once you find those scriptures suited for your situation, turn those scriptures into declarations. According to Job 22:28,

"You will also decide and decree a thing and it will be established" (Job 22:28 AMP).

"Thou shalt also decree a thing, and it shall be established unto you" (Job 22:28 KJV).

Context: As you declare God's word over your issue, you can be assured that your situation will turn around. Some of you may not be familiar with writing declarations or devising strategies based on the word of God. Don't fret. Below are examples of declarations that are verbatim from scripture and declarations that are specific to specific situations, but scripture based. As you get comfortable composing declarations and strategies, it will become easier.

Example1:

Scripture: "And from his fullness we have all received and grace up on grace" (John 1:15 BSB).

Declaration: I declare and decree from His fullness, I have received grace upon grace in Jesus name.

Example 1, is an illustration of declaring the scripture verbatim, but making it personal to you.

Example 2:

Scripture: "And from his fullness we have all received and grace upon grace" (John 1:15 BSB).

Declaration: I declare and decree from the fullness of Jesus Christ that I have received grace upon grace to fulfill the assignment of teaching and equipping God's people in Jesus name.

Example 2 illustrates a declaration that is targeted at a specific situation, actually my personal situation.

Personal Note:

As I am writing this book inspired by God, sharing specific strategies of the things I personally do when life happens outside of my family, and friends is a new assignment, although I have applied this strategy to my life for many years. God has inspired and pushed me to share this knowledge with all those who may need some guidance on how to handle life when curveballs or attacks come about. When I am about to enter into anything new, I always declare where I am headed. This strategy can be applied to situations, whether present or future.

Declarations are like prayers in statement form. Declarations are unique in that they serve as statements that speak or declare the solution or answer. Now that you understand the role of declarations and how they are constructed, you need to create a divine plan to apply the solution to your problem.

Step 7: Apply/Implement the Solution Strategically

In order to strategically implement Steps 1-6, you need to do the following:

- **Declare/Speak Your Declarations (Solutions)**
- **Worship**
- **Fast**

Declare/Speak Your Declarations (Solutions)

As discussed in step six, declaring the word of God over a problem is one of the key points in implementing divine strategy. Also, while declaring, you should worship.

Worship

Implementing worship is a vital aspect of divine strategy. As you worship, you express your adoration and reverence to God, which ushers in the Holy Spirit. Wherever the spirit of God resides, so does life, liberty, abundance, healing, and everything we need. Isaiah 61:1 is an excellent example that describes the benefits of the anointing of God being present.

"The spirit of the Lord God is upon me because the Lord has anointed and qualified me to preach the gospel of good tidings to the meek, the poor, and afflicted. He has sent me to build up and heal the brokenhearted to proclaim liberty to the [physical and spiritual] captives and the opening of prison and the eyes of those who are bound" (Isaiah 61:1 AMP).

Context: Inviting the Holy Spirit through worship as you are declaring creates an atmosphere that is conducive for transforming issues, overcoming matters of life, and experiencing real change. Another impactful spiritual element that should be incorporated along with this powerful combination is fasting.

Fasting

Fasting is another strategic component of divine strategy. Fasting is an effective spiritual tool that is sacrificial in nature, in which we abstain from food, water, or other pleasantries. As you fast, you draw closer to God by bringing your flesh under subjection as your spiritual abilities increase. As God strengthens your spiritual stamina through fasting, situations will turn in your favor; doors that were once closed will now open, and the impossible will become possible. A powerful example of the results of fasting can be found in Esther 3:13, Esther 4:16, and Esther 5:2-3.

The Problem

"And letters were sent by special messengers to all king's provinces-to destroy, to slay and to do away with all Jews, both young and old, little children and women, in one day, the thirteenth day of the twelfth month, the month of Adar, and to seize their belongings as spoils" (Esther 3:13 AMP).

The Solution

"Go gather together all the Jews that are present in Shushan, and fast for me, and neither eat nor drink for three days, night or day. I also and my maids will fast as you do. Then I will go to the king, though it is against the law, and if I perish, I perish" (Esther 4:16 AMP).

The Result

"[2] And when the king saw Esther the queen standing in the court, she obtained favor in his sight, and he held out to [her] the gold scepter that was in his hand. So Esther drew near and touched the tip of the scepter.[3] then the king said to her. What will you have, Queen Esther? What is your request? It shall be given you, even to the half of the kingdom" (Esther 5:2-3 AMP).

Context: Being intentional in pursuing God's presence through fasting moves God's heart and opens the door for blessings and favor. Implementing fasting as you make your petitions by declaration and reverence through worship produces a spiritual trifecta that is unmatched.

Conclusion

God never intended for you to live in defeat, worry, or fear. In fact, God has equipped you with spiritual tools so that you may possess a life of victory, faith, and peace. So, whenever situations arise, you can apply the spiritual principles of prayer by declaration, worship, and fasting to overcome the difficulties of life.

Personal Note:

On the next page, you will find a personal example of what divine strategy looks like and includes directions.

Divine Strategy

Date: 11-10-2020

Fast: November 10, 2020 – November 11, 2020

Nuts, fruit, and veggies ONLY (the sacrifice)

Purpose: The purpose of this fast is to go from transition to possession of the promises of God. As God led Joshua to take possession of the Promised Land, so shall it be unto me in Jesus name.

Declarations:

I declare and decree that my enemies' hearts shall melt in fear as the Amorite kings heard how you, Lord, dried up the Jordan before the Israelites in Jesus name (Joshua 2:11).

I declare and decree that my enemies' hearts shall melt in fear as the Amorite kings heard how you, Lord, dried up the Jordan before the Israelites in Jesus name (Joshua 2:11).

I declare that as the Israelites were circumcised, so it has been done unto me, and you God have removed all reproach, that I may eat the good of the land in Jesus name (Joshua 5:2-12).

Directions

- Write down the dates of your fast, how long it will be, and what the fast will consist of.

- Writing it down gives you a visual context of what you expect God to do, and you can watch it unfold before your eyes.

- Record the purpose of your fast. Basically, what do you seek from God? What situation do you desire God to change?

- Find scriptures related to the purpose of your fast and make declarations specific to your situation.

- If you are new to fasting, start off gradually and build up to longer times and periods as you fast consistently. Ex. Fast and abstain from meats and sweets from 8 am-12 pm (4 hours).

- Daily, start with worship or worship music, then start declaring, and end it with worship and thanking God for what He has done.

- While fasting, saturate yourself with the word of God, limit your television and social media, try not to argue or have strife with anyone, and focus on the things of God.
- Let the Holy Spirit lead you in all aspects of implementing the divine strategy. All you have to do is ask.

Glossary of Declarations

Anger

- I declare I shall not be quick in my spirit to become angry nor lodge anger in my heart in Jesus name. (Ecclesiastes 7:9)

- I declare I shall not be angry or sin, nor shall I let the sun go down on my anger in Jesus name. (Ephesians 4:26)

Anxiety and Worry

- I declare I shall cast all of my cares upon you, Oh God, for you care for me in Jesus name. (1 Peter 5:7)

- I declare that when I am in distress, I will call on you, Lord, and you will answer me in Jesus name. (Psalm 86:7)

Courage

- I declare and decree I shall wait for the Lord and be strong and courageous in Jesus name. (Psalm 27:14)

- I declare and decree I shall stand firm and let nothing move me and give myself fully to the work of the Lord, for my labor is in the Lord and is not in vain in Jesus name. (1 Corinthians 15:58)

Depression

- I declare I shall not be depressed, for you, Lord, are a shield around me, my glory, the One who lifts my head high. (Psalm 3:3)
- I declare and decree I shall arise and shine, for your light has come, and the glory of the Lord rises upon me in Jesus name. (Isaiah 60:1)

Faith

- I declare I shall take up the shield of faith, and all the flaming arrows of the evil one shall be extinguished in Jesus name. (Ephesians 6:16)
- I declare and decree that you, oh God, the God of hope, shall fill me with all joy and peace as I trust in you so that

I may overflow with hope by the power of the Holy Spirit in Jesus name. (Romans 15:13)

Fear

- I declare that I shall have a spirit of fear, but I shall walk in power, love, and a sound mind in Jesus name. (2 Timothy 1:7)
- I declare that as I walk through the darkest valley, I shall fear no evil because you, God, are with me and your rod and staff comfort me in Jesus name. (Psalm 23:4)

Healing and Health

- I decree I am healed because you, Lord God, heal the brokenhearted and bind my wounds in Jesus name. (Psalm 147:3)
- I declare and decree as you heal me, Lord, I am healed, and as you save me, I am saved for you are the One I praise in Jesus name. (Jeremiah 17:14)

Patience

- I declare and decree I shall not grow weary in well doing, for in season I will reap and harvest if I faint not in Jesus name. (Galatians 6:9)

- I declare I shall wait patiently upon the Lord, and you shall turn toward me and hear my cry in Jesus name. (Psalm 40:1)

Peace

- I declare I shall have peace because you have left and given me your peace, and my heart shall not be troubled or afraid in Jesus name. (John 14:27)

- I declare and decree that the peace of God that surpasses all understanding shall guard my heart and mind in Christ Jesus. (Philippians 4:7)

Protection

- I declare and decree I shall not fear because you, God, are with me and I shall not be dismayed because you are my God and you strengthen and help me and hold me up with your victorious right hand in Jesus name. (Isaiah 41:10)

- I declare and decree that you, Lord, are my refuge and strength; you are my ever-present help in the times of trouble in Jesus name. (Psalm 46:1)

Wisdom

- I declare I shall love wisdom and never forsake it because wisdom will protect and watch over me in Jesus name. (Proverbs 4:6)

- I declare and decree that I shall listen to advice and accept discipline, and I shall be counted among the wise at the end, in Jesus name. (Proverbs 19:20)

Dedication/Re-Dedication Prayer

The most important relationship you will ever form and develop is with Jesus Christ. If you have not dedicated or surrendered your life to Christ or maybe you haven't served God as you once did before I encourage you to say the prayer below.

Gracious Father, I come before you repenting of my sins, I believe your son Jesus Christ, died for my sins, was resurrected from the dead, and is alive. I surrender my will to you and invite Jesus Christ to become Lord over my life, to rule and reign in my heart from this day forward. Send your Holy Spirit to dwell within me that I may obey you, and do your will in Jesus mighty name I pray.

Amen

Now that you have dedicated or rededicated your life to Christ I encourage you to read the following books of the bible to get closer to the Lord by getting to know him.

Matthew

Mark

Luke

John

NOTES

NOTES

NOTES

NOTES

NOTES

NOTES

NOTES

NOTES

NOTES

NOTES

NOTES

NOTES

NOTES

NOTES

Made in the USA
Columbia, SC
06 April 2023

14529126R00028